THE ONE CALLED JESUS

A COLLECTION OF POETRY

Other Books by Sheri A. Sutton

And So It Is

The Light of Christmas

In Remembrance of Me

Memorable Moments

40 Days

Songs of Faith and Hope

THE ONE CALLED JESUS

A COLLECTION OF POETRY

SHERI A. SUTTON

THE ONE CALLED JESUS

A COLLECTION OF POETRY

© Sheri A. Sutton

ISBN: 978-0-9984548-5-6

Sheri A. Sutton
2 Callie Ct.
Wichita Falls, Texas 76310
United States of America
www.sheriasutton.com

In Loving Memory of

Shirley Frances Craft

whose friendship enriched my life.

For God so loved the world that He gave His only begotten Son, that whoever believes in Him should not perish but have everlasting life.

John 3:16 (NKJV)

TABLE OF CONTENTS

ACKNOWLEDGMENTS

With deepest appreciation to Dr. David Hartman for his continued friendship and support as well as his substantive and theological review of this work.

With sincere gratitude to Geneva Rodgers, dear friend and fellow poet, for her editorial review of this work.

INTRODUCTION

For many, Jesus signifies the Christ, the Son of the living God, and the long awaited Messiah. To others, he is a historical figure who changed the life of many because of his teachings. Regardless of philosophies or beliefs, there is no denying that throughout history no other person has impacted the world to the extent as the one called Jesus.

The Name

According to the Hebrew translation of the name Jesus (Yehoshua), it is a combination of two elements. One element translates as God (Yahweh); the other element means to deliver, save, or rescue (yasha). In that context, the name Jesus conveys the idea that God delivers or saves through the one who bears his name. Recorded in the book of Isaiah, the Christ-child would be called Immanuel, meaning "God with us".

Even for those who believe that Jesus is the long awaited Messiah, one great debate over the centuries has been the idea that he was fully human and fully divine. The psalmist often wrote of the longing for God's presence in his life, and Scripture tells us that God also longed for a relationship with his creation. Jesus, God in the flesh, was ready to live among us, to experience our humanness, and to give his life for all mankind.

The Birth

As recorded in the books of Matthew and Luke, Jesus' birth was anything but ordinary. He was conceived by the Holy Spirit and born to the Virgin Mary who was betrothed to a man named Joseph. Mary and Joseph were God's chosen to bring Jesus into the world. With great courage, they followed God's will against all odds and traditional values of the time.

Luke 2:1-7 reveals that in the first century Caesar Augustus issued a decree for a census to be taken of the entire Roman world. To participate, everyone had to register in their own town. Because Joseph belonged to the house and line of David, he and Mary went to Bethlehem.

By all appearances, it was an ordinary night—a family traveling to Bethlehem to register for the census. When they arrived, both were tired and weary from the trip. Joseph searched for a place to rest and found only a stable—a humble beginning for the Son of God. Amid the hay, the animals, and the stench, God chose to reveal himself to mankind as a baby. There were no big crowds, no bands playing, no confetti, and no banquet set for a king.

Chapter 2 of Luke's gospel continues in verses eight through twenty with the story of the shepherds who were living in the fields by Bethlehem. An angel appeared with the news of the birth, "Today in the town of David a Savior has been born to you" (v. 11). Although the shepherds were taken back by the news, they hurried to Bethlehem. Finding the baby, Mary, and Joseph, they quickly spread the news about the child, and everyone who heard it was amazed.

In Matthew's gospel, there is the account of the Magi in chapter 2. Several months after Jesus was born, these men came from the East to Jerusalem. Following a star in the heavens, they were searching for "the one who has been born king of the Jews" (v. 2). When they reached Bethlehem, they presented treasured gifts to the child and worshipped him.

Jesus' entrance into the world was no small matter. He was soon sought after by King Herod, who threatened by Jesus' birth and the possible downfall of his own kingship, ordered the killing of all boys in Bethlehem and surrounding vicinity who were two years old and under. Fortunately, warned by an angel in a dream, Joseph escaped with his family to Egypt and stayed there until Herod's death.

Not much is revealed about Jesus as a young boy, but scripture does give us some insights in Luke 2:22-52. By Jewish law, there were two ritual acts required for Jewish parents. One was the purification of the mother. The other was the redemption of the firstborn son which required a sacrifice. By law, this sacrifice could be a pair of turtledoves or two young pigeons for those who could not afford a sheep. Mary and Joseph lived according to the sacred law of Israel and journeyed to Jerusalem as required.

While in the temple, they encountered Simeon and Anna, two prophets who were righteous and devout. Upon seeing the baby Jesus, both spoke about the promised salvation of God's people. And according to Scripture, Simeon even indicated to Mary that "a sword will pierce through your own soul" (v. 35). Although they did not fully understand, Joseph and Mary marveled at all that was said.

Keeping with tradition, the family journeyed annually to Jerusalem for the Feast of the Passover. On one particular trip, Jesus was twelve years old. While traveling home after the last day of the Passover, Mary and Joseph realized Jesus was not in the company of relatives and friends. Upon their return to Jerusalem, they found him at the temple.

According to verse 49, Jesus stated "Why did you seek me? Did you not know that I must be about my Father's business?" Following verses tell us that Mary and Joseph were confused by these words.

However, as noted at the end of the chapter, Jesus did return to Nazareth and was obedient to Mary and Joseph. In addition, he grew in stature and became strong, gained wisdom, and found favor with God and man.

The Baptism

Baptism, for Christian believers, is a ritual for those who profess their faith in Jesus Christ symbolizing the death of one's old self and the birth of a new self in Christ. Although it may appear odd that Jesus took part in this type of ritual, all four gospels include Jesus' baptism in the Jordan River.

In Matthew 3, John the Baptist was certainly surprised. He tried to deter Jesus by saying, "I need to be baptized by you, and do you come to me?" (v. 14). Jesus was adamant, and, after his baptism, the Spirit of God descended on him like a dove. "And a voice from heaven said, 'This is my Son, whom I love; with him I am well pleased' " (v. 17).

Matthew 3:15 records Jesus' baptism as necessary for the fulfillment of all righteousness. Luke 3:23 tells us that at the age of thirty this ritual of baptism marked the beginning of Jesus' ministry.

The Temptation

After his baptism, Matthew 4:1-11 and Luke 4:1-13 give us detailed accounts of Jesus' time in the wilderness. He fasted for forty days and nights and was hungry according to Scripture. The enemy considered him an easy target as he tempted Jesus with worldly rewards. However, during the fasting, the practice of prayer and meditation had strengthened Jesus to overcome the enemy's bait by using the principles found in Scripture.

When Jesus was tempted with food, he countered with "man cannot live by bread alone." When his identity was questioned, he replied "do not put the Lord your God to the test." Finally, when Jesus was offered all the kingdoms of the world, he responded, "worship the Lord your God, and serve him only." Although the enemy used Scripture (e.g. Psalm 91:11-12) to entice Jesus, he was unsuccessful. For every untruth, Jesus used the power of Holy Scripture to expose the enemy's scheme.

The Calling

All four gospels include details of Jesus calling his first disciples. According to Scripture, Peter, Andrew, and the sons of Zebedee, James and John, were the first disciples. These men left their livelihoods and their families to follow Jesus. As he told them in Luke 5:10, "Don't be afraid; from now on you will fish for people."

In that period of history, discipleship was a well-known aspect of Judaism because it contained a definite system for teaching. The student or disciple lived with his teacher to share his experiences as well as to learn his teachings. In addition, the disciple was expected to take these teachings as a pattern for living. Lastly, discipleship was designed to shape the character and thinking of the student. Jesus used this teaching style with the twelve disciples to prepare them to spearhead a missionary movement of the gospel message that still empowers people around the world today.

* * *

Jesus healed many people and taught many lessons through parables and personal interaction in his three-year ministry. It is impossible to include the totality of his ministry in one book. Therefore, in *The One Called Jesus*, forty poems written in free verse form offer the reader only a glimpse into this exceptional life—a life filled with God's love, mercy, and redemption.

One might wonder about using a collection of poetry to explore the ministry of Jesus as compared to other types of writing. Poetry expresses ideas in a compact precise way,

5

leaving out unnecessary words and ideas. It drills down to a snapshot of a moment in time as imagined through the eyes of the poet.

It is the author's sincere hope that the reader will gain a new perspective from these snapshots of the extraordinary ministry of Jesus and the continuous impact of his life, death, and resurrection on our lives still today.

POEMS

All poems in this book are based on specific readings from the Gospels as recorded in the New International Version (NIV) of the Bible. Within these poems, quotation marks and/or italics are used to indicate dialogue and do not necessarily imply a direct quote from the NIV.

WATER TO WINE
John 2:1-11

Wedding bliss—
love saturates the air.
Invited guests gather,
including Jesus and his disciples.
Joyful celebration, food and wine overflow.

Jesus watches from a distance.
Bride and groom begin new life—
total trust, complete joy.

His mother's voice interrupts,
"There is no more wine."
She does not understand—
his hour has not come.
Her world is here,
his is elsewhere.

He sighs. To the servants,
	"Fill these jars with water, then serve."
Tradition provides choice wine first—
here, the best saved for last.
An extravagant gesture!

Jesus watches from a distance.
There is much to do. He signals
his disciples; their journey begins.

NICODEMUS
John 3:1-8

Shroud of darkness
eases the danger—
seeking Jesus is risky.

Declaring his
connection to God,
insane for respected
Pharisee leader.

Their conversation fuels
a simple question,
"How can I be born again?
I cannot enter my mother's womb."

> *"You do not understand—*
> *flesh gives birth to flesh,*
> *but Spirit gives birth to spirit."*

DRAWING WATER FROM THE WELL
John 4:1-30, 39-42

Noon—sun's brutally hot.
Her body sweats,
only foolish women
draw water this time of day.
She prefers solitude,
no judgment from others.
She squints—someone is there.

Tired, thirsty, his journey long,
Jesus waits at Jacob's well.
 "May I have a drink?"
She is perplexed—
he is Jewish, she a Samaritan.
"Why do you ask me for water?"
 "If you knew me, you would ask
 for living water."

With utter disbelief,
"How can you give me water?
The well is deep, you have no bucket."
 "This water does not quench
 your thirst. But whoever drinks
 my water will never thirst."

She peers deep into his eyes.
He knows her completely.
"Are you a prophet?
Is the Messiah coming?"
 "Your wait is over. I am the Messiah."
She drops her water jar, runs to town.

Breathless, she shares her story.
"He told me everything I ever did!"
Pausing, she asks slowly,
deliberately, "Do you think...
could he be...the Messiah?"
Many, touched by her words,
believed immediately.

Others rush to find him.
Truth pierces their hearts,
"We have heard him and
seen him; therefore, we believe
he is the Savior of the world."
For many the question lingers,
could Jesus be...?

LEPER
Mark 1:40–45

Dreaded disease—
leper unclean, excluded,
void of touch or love.
He searches for Jesus.
On bended knee,
 "You can cleanse me
if you are willing."

Ravaging effects of disease
anger Jesus. With compassion,
 "I am willing. Be clean!"
Immediately, man's body
is healed, whole, transformed.
 "Say nothing, but offer sacrifices."

Restored, he talks freely,
despite Jesus' command.
News spreads rapidly.
Like a raging fire across the land,
enormous crowds from far and near
gather to listen to the one called Jesus.
Even in remote places, there is no rest.

FORGIVEN AND HEALED
Luke 5:17-26

They come from everywhere—
Galilean villages, Judea,
Jerusalem to catch a glimpse,
to hear a word, to be healed.
Skeptics, Pharisees, teachers
of the law watch the crowd,
watch Jesus.

Friends carry paralyzed man—
unable to walk, needs healing.
They maneuver toward Jesus,
but no access. Filled with despair,
they look up—the roof!
They lower the man for healing.
Courageous persistence,
faith in action.

    "Friend, your sins are forgiven."
Shouts of blasphemy fill the air.
Jesus knows their minds—forgiveness of sin
only from God. To the man,
    "Get up, take your mat, and go home."
Forgiveness heals body, mind, and spirit—
no longer paralyzed, he stands in grateful praise.

UNCHAINED POWER
Matthew 8:5–13

Roman centurion, known
as a godly man, seeks help—
his servant, paralyzed
with unbearable pain.
He finds Jesus.

"Please, please heal my servant,"
    "Shall I go to him?"
Head bows, "I am not deserving.
Speak and he will be healed."

Jesus marvels—the man's
faith like none other.
        "Go! It will be done
        just as you believe."

Jesus' mercy, not bound
by circumstances
or preconceptions.
Healing power, not chained
by time or distance.

IN THE VILLAGE OF NAIN
Luke 7:11-17

As she walks, she grieves.
A lowly widow, her only son dead.
What would she do now?
She takes slow, uncertain steps.

Squelching sun bears down.
Funeral procession passes
through the village gate.
Tears spill over her face.

Jesus and his disciples
approach the village.
His heart touched,
"Do not cry."

He stops the bearers.
"Young man, get up!"
The son sits up, begins to speak.
Jesus returns the son to his mother.

All present amazed
by the unexpected miracle.
God present and active,
in real life and real time.

WOMAN OF SIN
Luke 7:36–50

Jesus accepts Pharisee's
dinner invitation.
Uninvited woman arrives,
deemed sinful by many.
Stands behind Jesus—
invited guests indignant.

With her tears
she washes Jesus' feet;
her hair, a towel for drying.
Her lips caress his feet;
expensive perfume soothes them.
Pharisee scowls.

> *"You did not give
> water to clean my feet,
> she gave her tears.
> You did not offer a kiss,
> she kissed my feet.
> You did not anoint my head,
> she covered my feet with oil
> she could not afford."*

He knows the woman's heart.
> *"Your sins are forgiven.
> You are saved by faith,
> now go in peace."*
Love and forgiveness equally important
when transforming lives.

FEAR BLINDS THE TRUTH
Mark 4:35–41

To his disciples,
> *"Let us go to the other side."*

Tired and weary from large crowds,
Jesus sleeps in boat's stern.

Suddenly, a powerful storm develops.
Waves crash, water fills the boat.
Fear overwhelms the disciples.
"Teacher, wake up! Help us or we'll drown!"

> *"Quiet! Be still!"*

Wind dies, water calms.
> *"Why are you fearful?*
> *Where is your faith?"*

Who is this they ponder?
Fear blinds the truth.
In time, awareness leads
to revelation—faith, the result.

WHO TOUCHED ME?
Luke 8:42b–48

Wherever he goes,
crowds surround him.
Today is no exception—
many want healing, mercy, love.
Jesus walks forward.

Ill from many years of bleeding,
a woman follows the crowd,
hopeful of a miracle.
Doctors offer no cure—
he is her last stop.

She moves forward,
only an arms-length away.
Desperate measures—
she stoops, stretches her arm,
touches the hem of his cloak.

Jesus stops abruptly.
    "Who touched me?"
The people crowd around—
he studies their faces.
    "Who touched me?"

She cannot hide. Trembling, she falls
at his feet and tells her story. He listens—
the bleeding, the doctors, the rejection.
No one had helped her. No one could.
    "Daughter, your faith has healed you.
    Go in peace."

WHAT IS SUFFICIENT?
Matthew 14:13-21

Remote surroundings—
Jesus needs rest
but crowds follow,
most on foot.

He feels compassion
and heals many.
Late afternoon,
disciples insist
on dismissal of crowd.
"No food," they argue.

> *"Give them food,"*
he counters. They hesitate—
five loaves of bread, two fish,
insufficient for massive crowd.

Jesus blesses
the meager offering,
then breaks the loaves.
More than five thousand
men, women, and children fed.
Twelve full baskets remain.

Bread and fish satisfy
a temporary hunger,
while their spirits cry out
for the bread of life.

STORMY WATERS
Matthew 14:22–33

Weary and worn,
Jesus seeks solitude—
sends disciples across the lake.
On mountainside, he prays.

Shortly before dawn,
he walks across the water.
Disciples watch ghostly silhouette
moving toward the boat.
    "It is me. Do not be afraid."

"Tell me to come to you," Peter demands.
    "Come."
He steps out. Seized by fear,
he quickly sinks. "Lord, save me!"

    "You of little faith."
Jesus grabs Peter's hand.
Wind stills, all is quiet. Fear relieved.
"Truly, you are the Son of God!"

For some, faith is assurance
strengthened by proof.
For others, courageous anxiety—
daring to believe God with us
in the storms of life.

UNCLEAN HEART
Mark 7:1-23

Pharisees ready to set
another trap for Jesus—
his disciples eat
with unclean hands.
Old traditions broken.

Pharisees hope
he answers foolishly.
Jesus recognizes the trap
and responds.

> *"Is human tradition greater*
> *than God's commands?*
> *Unclean hands do not defile*
> *the body. But an unclean heart?*
> *That is a different story."*

Nothing outside defiles a person,
only what comes from inside.
Beware, humanity's stumbling block—
an impure heart.

WHO DESERVES HEALING?
Matthew 15:21-28

Weary from crowds, Jesus withdraws to Tyre.
Canaanite woman approaches,
distressed and desperate, in need of help.
Daughter is demon-possessed.

Jesus does not acknowledge her hardship.
He has come for the lost Israelites,
not non-Jews. How can he help her
when so many of his own need healing?

> *"Do you want me to toss*
> *the children's bread to the dogs."*

Her heart breaks for her child—
she knows prejudice against Gentiles.
With courage, "Even the dogs eat the crumbs
that fall under the table."

> *"You of great faith!"*

In an instant, her daughter is healed.
Barriers broken, perceptions changed.
God's message of mercy and grace
extends beyond human boundaries.

HEAR AND SPEAK
Mark 7:31-37

In the region of Decapolis,
friends bring a man,
deaf and mute, to Jesus.
They beg for his healing.

Away from gathering crowds,
holy fingers into deaf ears,
spit for silent tongue.
Eyes on heaven,
Jesus draws deep breath,
        "Be opened!"
In that moment, ears hear,
tongue speaks.

Limitations shattered.
Ability to hear and share
the good news paramount
to the transformation of the world.

CONFESSION OF FAITH
Matthew 16:13-20

"Who do people say I am?
The disciples reply, "Some say you are
John the Baptist raised to life.
Others, Elijah or perhaps a prophet."

"Peter, who do you say I am?"
"You are the Messiah,
the Son of the living God."

Personal confession of faith
in the one called Jesus.
Rock-strong and foundational
for building community of faith.

TRUE LIFE
Luke 9:21-27

The Son of Man—
suffering servant
rejected by many.
His mission misunderstood.

Does the world offer more?
The world tempts,
but does not fulfill.
Many easily lose their way.

Greed, power, separation, fear—
the world offers no hope
without love, mercy, and grace.

To have true life
one must lose their life.
Dying to self is required,
dismantling ego necessary.

Revelation and transformation
not an easy path.
The result, a life of substance—
a life resurrected into the light.

WHO IS THE GREATEST?
Matthew 18:1-5

They want to know.
"Please tell us,
who is the greatest
in God's kingdom?"

Jesus' disciples,
perplexed and over-ambitious.
Human nature always lurks,
waiting for a misstep.

Jesus embraces a child.
    "Change your ways,
    become like this child.
    The kingdom of heaven awaits."

A child,
a lowly child?
Humility, trust—
change and begin anew.

    "Who welcomes one child, welcomes me."
Simple, straight forward, and difficult.
Human nature demands hidden agendas,
selfishness, and status.

Jesus' teachings call for change—
a reset, a radical transformation of thought,
an unexpected pattern for living.
The result, heaven on earth.

THE ADULTERESS
John 7:53-8:11

People gather in the Temple courts
anxious to hear Jesus teach.
Teachers of the law and Pharisees,
intimidated by his popularity,
contrive a plan of entrapment.

An adulterous woman
stands before the group—
head bowed, ashamed, and frightened.
Stoning, the severe penalty by law.

To Jesus, "What do you say is her punishment?"
Silence as Jesus moves his finger in the dirt.
Questions continue.
He straightens with authority,

> *"Who is without sin, throw the first stone."*
He stoops, writes again in the sand.
One by one the accusers leave,
the woman stands alone with Jesus.

> *"Who condemns you?"*
Eyes lowered, "No one, "she says quietly.
> *"Neither do I. Go and sin no more."*
Forgiveness—set free from guilt and shame,
and called to an honorable life.

BORN BLIND
John 9:1-12

Jesus sees the man,
blinded at birth.
He makes mud
with spit and dirt,
rubs it on eyes.

> *"Go, wash your eyes."*
The man returns with sight restored.
Many wary of healing miracle,
incredible yet unbelievable.

Dirt from dry ground,
spit from Jesus' mouth.
How could this be?
From the ordinary to extraordinary,
God's unexpected healing style.

Many cannot see God
in the ordinary or miraculous.
Only light of awareness
brings sight to the blind.

MARTHA AND MARY
Luke 10:38-42

The news is clear—
Jesus will visit the little village.
Martha begins preparations.
Support for Jesus and
his mission is her priority.
So many details to organize,
so little time.

When he arrives, Martha welcomes him
but continues with her tasks.
Mary, the younger sister, sits at Jesus' feet.
Confident in her choice to listen and learn,
she devours every word.
Martha is hurt—why doesn't Mary
help instead of wasting time?

Jesus clearly sees the situation.
A rivalry of sorts—two sisters,
two different perspectives.
One offers hospitality by doing,
the other by being.
The outcome for both—
the gift of being with the Master.

LAZARUS, COME OUT!
John 11:1-44

Death of Lazarus—
difficult for family,
Mary and Martha
grieve their brother's death.

More challenging,
Jesus doesn't come.
"He could have healed
our brother," they cry.

Laid in a tomb, four days pass.
Nothing can help him now.
The loss, the tears,
the grief overwhelms.

Jesus comes but not when expected.
He feels their pain,
disappointment, questions.
He weeps.

Death is not the end...
　　　"Remove the stone," Jesus commands.
　　　"Come out!" Lazarus walks out.
　　　"Take off the grave clothes, let him go!"

For Jesus, timing significant.
Not Mary and Martha's schedule,
only his timing. When least expected,
God's power overcomes and restores.

TRUE WEALTH
Mark 10:17-31

"Teacher," asks the man,
"how do I receive eternal life?"
  "You know the commandments."
"Of course, I keep them always."
  "Then sell your belongings,
  give away the money, and follow me."
The man leaves with a grieving heart.

Possessions, money, prestige
falsely offer us power, security,
success, and happiness.
Worldly ways, wolves waiting for prey.

Holding tightly breeds
greed, selfishness, fear.
Life becomes a prison and
kills God's created masterpiece.
Jesus offers much more than the world—
the gift of true life filled with freedom, joy,
love, forgiveness, mercy, and grace.

ZACCHAEUS
Luke 19:1-10

Rich tax collector, dreaded by all,
assumed dishonest by most.
He desperately wants
to see Jesus, but large crowd
obstructs his view.

A sycamore tree ahead,
he runs and climbs the tree.
As Jesus walks, he looks up.
> *"Zacchaeus, come down.*
> *Take me to your house."*

Many in the crowd shake their heads.
By all standards disgraceful,
Jesus the guest of a sinner.
Zacchaeus does not run or hide
but stands with confidence,
his eyes on the one he came to see.

"I will give half of all I have to the poor.
For those I have cheated, I will repay
four times the amount."
> *"Today salvation is yours. The Son of Man*
> *comes to seek and save the lost."*

The journey of faith, following Jesus.
Through Jesus, God seeks those
who are lost, alone, afraid, unloved,
vulnerable, outcast, and forgotten.
God's plan, salvation for all.

ANOINTED
John 12:1-8

It is a simple story of love.
Jesus and disciples visit
Lazarus, Martha, Mary.
Martha serves dinner,
an honorable feast
for their special friend.

Mary pours expensive perfume,
often used for burial,
to wash Jesus' feet.
Fragrant scent fills the air.

Judas, keeper of money
and soon to be betrayer,
indignantly voices
wasteful use of resources.
Purchase of expensive perfume
or assistance for poor and needy?

With compassion, Jesus replies,
>*"Leave her alone.*
>*You will always have the poor,*
>*but my time is limited."*

Crucifixion, burial, resurrection,
no comprehension by disciples.
But Mary, sweet Mary,
understands. When she wipes
the Master's feet with her hair,
tears fill her eyes.

A Servant's Heart
John 13:1-17

His hour has come.
He will leave this world,
and those he loves.

Disciples gather around
table for evening meal.
His eyes capture the moment.

Jesus pours water into a basin
to wash their feet. For drying,
a towel around his waist.

This act of ancient hospitality
usually performed by slaves.
He moves from disciple to disciple.

At first, Peter rejects
this act of servant love.
Soon, he will understand.

> *"No servant greater than his master.*
> *I have set an example for you.*
> *Do what I have done."*

In Remembrance of Me
Matthew 26:26-29

Arrangements set.
Jesus and his twelve
gather for Passover meal.

Jesus blesses and breaks the bread,
>   *"Take and eat. This is my body.*
>   *Do this in remembrance of me."*

Bread nourishes the body.
Jesus, the Bread of Life,
offers life eternal.

He pours and blesses the wine,
>   *"Drink. This is my blood given for many.*
>   *Do this in remembrance of me."*

Jesus offers himself—
the new covenant
poured out for many.

His betrayer hides among the twelve.
Soon, Jesus will become
the sacrificial lamb for all.

A PRAYER FOR ALL
John 17

He brings good news.
God's kingdom is near—
love, forgiveness, mercy for all.
Many accept, many deny.

An arduous assignment
calling disciples, teaching, healing.
So much to accomplish, too little time.

The end is close. Last hours in prayer,
> *"The hour has come. Protect and
> sanctify all to complete unity."*

Unity of purpose is common goal.
Surrender empowers life,
fullness of faith the result.
Oneness with God revealed.

GETHSEMANE
Matthew 26:36-46

He feels deep sorrow in his spirit.
Overwhelmed, he aches
for solitude, for peace.
His time on earth nears completion.

He takes Peter, James, and John
to keep watch for those
who will come.
On his knees he falls,
"Father, take this cup!"

When he returns to the disciples,
he finds them asleep.
"Watch and pray to resist temptation!"
He goes a second and third time to pray,
again the men asleep and unaware.

The hour has come,
"Father, your will be done."
Soldiers approach the garden,
his betrayer leads the way.

BETRAYAL
Matthew 26:14-16, 47-56

Judas, one of the twelve,
keeper of money bag,
tempted by thirty silver coins.
In the garden of Gethsemane,
betrays Jesus with a kiss.

Soldiers and disciples—
tempers high, swords raised.
Jesus speaks with irritation.
"I am not leading a rebellion!
You had other opportunities to arrest me,
but you chose to come under the veil of darkness."

Jesus arrested, disciples flee.
He is tired, alone, deserted.
Sigh of desperation,
sigh of relief—the end is in sight,
fulfillment of purpose underway.

TRIED AND CONDEMNED
Mark 14:55-65

Sanhedrin seeks condemning evidence,
he stands before Caiaphas, the high priest.
To trap Jesus, false testimony,
relentless questions—he does not answer.

Conflicted evidence and accusations.
Nothing concrete to charge Jesus.
"Are you the Messiah, the Son of God?"
        "I am."

They charge him with blasphemy,
condemn him worthy of death.
Spit and fists show their disgust.
Blindfold, beatings, imprisonment.

Power and greed cause fear,
hate, misplaced judgment.
The journey to the cross continues,
God's purpose to be revealed.

PILATE
Luke 23:1-5, 13-25

Jewish religious leaders hurl false charges
and malicious lies—Jesus stirs the people
with his teachings, incites rebellion.

Pilate listens, finds no basis of guilt,
no reason for death. To appease unruly crowd,
he sentences Jesus for flogging and release.

Crowd commands release of Barabbas,
one convicted of insurrection. "Crucify Jesus!"
Three times, Pilate argues no grounds for death.

Loud, unstoppable cries challenge and incite.
Forced by raging crowd, Pilate surrenders.
Shouts of victory—an innocent man faces death.

WALK TO GOLGOTHA
Matthew 27:27-33

Mocked, stripped, beaten, flogged;
body bruised and covered in blood.
A scarlet robe, a crown of thorns,
soldiers lead Jesus to Golgotha,
the place of the Skull.

They force Simon of Cyrene
to help carry the cross.
The road is rough and rocky.
Weight of cross bears down
on Jesus' weak, torn body.

He stumbles, he falls.
People shout, people wail.
Some follow,
some ridicule,
some turn their heads.

The way is grueling, movement is slow.
Sun burns his broken bloody body,
the cross a heavy burden.
One man, the one called Jesus,
walks to Golgotha for all mankind.

CRUCIFIXION
Luke 23:32-43

Soldiers lay him on the cross,
pound nails through hands and feet.
Head bows, breathing strenuous.
    "Father, forgive them."

Soldiers divide his clothes by lots.
People watch the spectacle, others sneer.
Soldiers mock him and offer sour wine.
A sign above, "The King of the Jews."

Two criminals hang on either side.
One ridicules Jesus, the other is reverent.
"Remember me when your kingdom comes."
    "Today you will be with me in paradise."

Jesus, the Son of God,
the long awaited Messiah,
hangs between man's doubt and fear
and God's abundant eternal love.

THREE HOURS OF DARKNESS
Mark 15:33-35

Noon, complete darkness
creeps over the land.
Jesus hangs on the cross,
his breathing labored,
his organs failing,
his skin tearing,
his death eminent.

Three hours pass, only silence.
A cry of anguish rumbles across the universe,
    "My God, my God,
      why have you forsaken me?"
A cry of doubt, of desperation,
of loss, of abandonment.
In the midst of pure evil, alone.

LAST MOMENTS
John 19:28-30, Luke 23:46

"I am thirsty."
Simple, straightforward,
a dying man's request.
Wine vinegar soaks into sponge.
Lifted to his lips, Jesus drinks.

"It is finished,"
the temple curtain splits.
A shout of completion,
"Father, into your hands
I commit my spirit."

He bows his head,
draws his last breath.
His body limp on the cross,
the suffering over.
Silence saturates the air.

Followers watch from a distance.
Many in the crowd grief stricken,
tears fall, hearts break.
Roman soldier speaks,
"Surely, this is a righteous man."

THE BURIAL
John 19:38-42

The crowd's roar reduces to a whisper.
Crying and wailing barely audible.
The spectacle over, quiet disbelief
and resignation fill the air.

Joseph of Arimathea asks for the body,
Nicodemus accompanies him.
A bold move considering the day's events.

They prepare Jesus for burial.
Strips of cloth, pounds of aloes and myrrh.
In silence, they wrap the body.
No time to waste, Sabbath begins soon.

The intensity requires no words.
Their breathing labored,
tears fill their sighs.

Do they relive the events of the day?
Do they recall his voice while tenderly
preparing his body? Finished, they lay
him in a tomb untouched by death.

Two followers perform an intimate,
grief-filled duty for their Master. Why?
He transformed their lives with his love.

THE TOMB
Matthew 27:62-66, 28:1

Pharisees and chief priests seek
audience with Pilate. Their fear—
Jesus' body will be stolen from the tomb.
    "After three days I will rise again,"
rings in their ears.
Pilate, manipulated once more,
consents to their request.

A soldier secures the tomb
by sealing the stone.
He stands guard,
two women watch from a distance.
Jesus' broken body, wrapped in linen,
lies in darkened tomb.
The weight of death hangs heavy.

HEAVEN AND EARTH COLLIDE
Matthew 28:2-10

Sunday morning dawns.
A violent earthquake
as heaven and earth collide.
An angel appears,
rolls the stone aside,
and rests on it.

His appearance resembles lightning,
his clothes, as white as snow.
The guards shake with fear,
becoming dead-like as statues.

The tomb is empty, no one inside.
The one called Jesus
not tied by the chains of man.
Released from the depths of hell,
the purpose of God manifests
as the gift of freedom for all.

HE IS RISEN!
John 20:11-18

Mary Magdalene stands weeping.
Where is my Lord? What have they done?
She turns and sees someone.
  "Why are you crying?"

She doesn't recognize him, perhaps the gardener?
"They have taken my Lord, but I don't know where."
  "Mary."
When Jesus whispers her name,
truth is revealed. She turns, "Teacher!"

The miracle of God's love, the power of resurrection.
The cross is bare, hope lies in the empty tomb—
the hope of victory over doubt and fear.
Jesus is risen! He is risen indeed!

AFTERWORD

When Jesus began his ministry, life on this planet changed forever. He associated with the marginalized of society, healed the sick, fed the poor, and acquired the reputation as a lawbreaker even though he urged obedience to the Law. Jesus did not come to overthrow the Roman government as many had hoped. He came to preach the good news—"Repent, for the kingdom of heaven has come near" (Matthew 4:17)—and to redeem the world through love as a sacrifice once for all.

The Appearances

Although women were marginalized in ancient society, they played an important role in the ministry of Jesus. When Mary Magdalene encountered the risen Christ at the tomb, Jesus told her to "go...and tell" (John 20:17). She went immediately to tell the disciples all that had happened.

Jesus appeared many more times to the disciples and followers. Another account is found in Luke 24:13-35. Two men on their way to Emmaus talked about all the things that had happened in Jerusalem. Jesus joined them on the road. Unrecognized, he asked what they were discussing. The men recounted the events surrounding the crucifixion and resurrection. As they approached a village, they urged Jesus to stay the night. During the evening meal, Jesus took the bread, broke it, and gave it to them. At that moment, they recognized him, and their hearts and minds were opened.

In addition, Jesus appeared to the disciples as recorded in John 20:19-29. "Peace be with you," he said. Thomas had his doubts. Jesus showed him the wounds in his hands and side. "Stop doubting and believe," he said. Then, Thomas believed because he had seen, and Jesus declared, "Blessed are those who have not seen and yet have believed."

The Commission

Matthew 28:18-20 gives us Jesus' final words to the disciples, his commission: "All authority in heaven and on earth has been given to me. Therefore go and make disciples of all nations, baptizing them in the name of the Father and of the Son and of the Holy Spirit, and teaching them to obey everything I have commanded you."

The Ascension

Scripture holds little information about Jesus' ascension. Luke 24:50-51 records, "When he had led them (*the disciples*) out to the vicinity of Bethany, he lifted up his hands and blessed them. While he was blessing them, he left them and was taken up into heaven." The Gospel of Mark has something similar in verses that scholars believe were added after the fact.

According to the more detailed description of the ascension in Acts 1:6-11, Jesus ascended in the presence of his disciples forty days after the resurrection. In the Old Testament, the Messiah ascended into the presence of the Ancient of Days (Daniel 7:13-14). For the New Testament, the ascension is the climax of the passion of Christ. As a dated event in the history of the world, it has lasting significance connecting God's heavenly kingdom with his kingdom to come on earth.

* * *

Much has been written concerning Jesus. Movies have tried to capture the essence of his life and ministry. Galleries are lined with artistic impressions of him, and hymnals fill church pews in order to bring the gospel alive in song. Still, all fall short. How can one adequately describe Jesus or his ministry?

It is believed that Napoleon once said, "Everything in Christ astonishes me. His spirit overawes me, and his will confounds me. Between him and whoever else in the world, there is no possible term of comparison. He is truly a being by himself...I search in vain in history to find the similar to Jesus Christ, or anything which can approach the gospel. Neither history, nor humanity, nor the ages, nor nature, offer me anything with which I am able to compare it or to explain it. Here everything is extraordinary."

Jesus and his ministry cannot be adequately described. He lived every day as an example of what he taught. His teachings were in opposition to the main religious thought of the time, and, as a result, he was persecuted and died the horrible death of crucifixion. His death, however, did not stop his message. With his resurrection came a resurgence of his ministry through the work of the apostles and followers.

When Paul and Barnabas created a church in Antioch and preached there for a year, the followers of the church were called "Christians" for the first time (Acts 11:26). In 380AD, Christianity became the official state religion of the Roman Empire. According to statistics today, 2.4 billion people of the world population identify as Christian.

The original disciples were a group of ordinary people who chose to be a part of something extraordinary. They were fearful, but they stepped out in faith. In John 21:15-17, Jesus asked Peter three times if he loved him. Of course, Peter answered that he did. Jesus remarked after each of Peter's answers either "feed my lambs", or "take care of my sheep", or "feed my sheep".

We, too, are asked to step out armed with faith and confidence to live an authentic life guided by the powerful ministry of the one called Jesus. This ministry of hope for all, fueled by God's eternal love and mercy, only continues when we choose to be the example of Jesus' healing presence in the world by following his teachings and his way of life. It is a simple request to all of us to change the world, "Take care of my sheep."

"Teacher, which is the greatest commandment in the Law?"

Jesus replied, "Love the Lord your God with all your heart and with all your soul and with all your mind. This is the first and greatest commandment. And the second is like it: Love your neighbor as yourself. All the Law and the Prophets hang on these two commandments."

Matthew 22:36-40

IN MEMORIAM

SHIRLEY

Devoted to God, family, country;
a faithful friend. A force of nature,
spirited, courageous, committed,
engaged. Willing to be of service;
her love, time, and talents
given generously.

This is the Shirley we know and love.
But today, we mourn her passing
in the aching of our hearts.
In time, the memories
we carry will comfort us,
photos we revisit will remind us,
and the love she gave will remain
forever in our hearts.

Through our tears, let us remember
her smile and the twinkle in her eye
that say to us:
      "I am still here.
      Smell the rose that blooms in the morning sun,
      feel the gentle rain on a summer afternoon,
      or gaze at the brightest star in the evening sky.
      I am in all these things.

      So don't cry for me.
      I am finally home,
      where I've always yearned to be,
      in the presence of the Master.
      All is well,
      all is well."

"And surely I am with you always, to the very end of the age."

Matthew 28:20

ABOUT THE AUTHOR

Sheri A. Sutton is an author, devotional writer, and poet. Her newest book, *The One Called Jesus*, is a collection of forty poems focusing on the ministry of Jesus. As a member of the Wichita Falls Poetry Society and the Poetry Society of Texas, Sutton has been recognized in various local and state contests. Her poetry has been published in her work, *Memorable Moments*, as well as the *Wichita Falls Literature and Art Review* and *The Secret Place* magazines, The Poetry Society of Texas' *A Book of the Year, Lifting the Sky, A Celebration of Poetry*, and the *2023 Texas Poetry Calendar*.

Sutton also has published five devotional books, and her devotional writing has been published in *The Secret Place* devotional magazine and the *Lenten Devotions on the Lord's Prayer*. Her work is found as well in the following Advent eBook devotional publications by First Christian Church, Wichita Falls, TX: *Calm and Bright, Chrismons*, and *He Is Called*.

For a limited time, Sutton wrote a monthly newspaper column while serving on the Community Editorial Board of the Times Record News.

Sutton offers professional services that include writing and editing for books, newsletters, and other materials for individuals, companies, or organizations. Fees are competitive within the industry.

In addition, she is available to share her faith and life experiences through public speaking, workshops, Bible studies, or other similar events. For more information, visit her website at www.sheriasutton.com.

Sutton and her husband, Lloyd Mark Sutton, live in Wichita Falls, Texas.